especially for

SUE

may your walls know joy...

may
your walls
know joy...

mary anne radmacher

Conari Press

First published in 2009 by
Red Wheel/Weiser, LLC
With offices at:
500 Third Street, Suite 230
San Francisco, CA 94107
www.redwheelweiser.com

ISBN: 978-1-57324-400-8
Library of Congress Cataloging-in-Publication Data
available upon request.

Cover and text design by Jessica Dacher
Typeset in Agenda

Printed in Hong Kong
GWP
10   9   8   7   6   5   4   3   2   1

For my home—David Lee Gordon

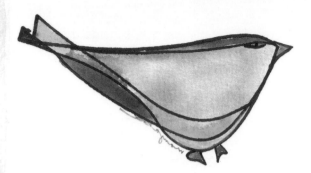

Some years ago I left Ireland after weeks of traveling throughout the island. I was a visitor, a stranger each place I went. Yet I never felt the stranger. Hospitality wrapped me in welcome, encouragement, and joy. I felt so "at home." I wanted to write a blessing that captured this spirit.

I did not remain lost any place in Ireland for very long. I loved hearing the inquiry prompted by my furrowed brow and puzzled look: "You lookin' fer yur way home, lass?" My way home. It is true that home is so much more than a building with a number we list on forms or licenses. Home happens in unexpected places and at unanticipated moments. Home can be a surprise at a new address.

Many years after writing the blessing that Ireland inspired (May your walls know joy . . .), I was excited to create a permanent home for myself. Discouragement set in after so many drive-arounds with my real estate agent. I *wanted* to see joy in the walls . . . I just didn't. That is, until one afternoon when I was steps inside a place. I heard my patient realtor whisper behind me, "I have a very good feeling about this . . ." "Home," I interrupted.

"Home. This is it. *This* is my home." It was a declaration.

My realtor understood that connecting with the intangibles of "home" is essentially like love at first sight. Who can explain that beyond a feeble, "I just knew"? An offer was delivered within an hour. Soon this blessing was a framed poster, hanging on a wall in my new home.

This book is what came of writing that blessing and my thoughts about it. This is a blessing for coming in and going out. A blessing for what happens on the inside of a home as much as the road away from and back to home. This is a blessing for the guest as well as the dweller. These wishes hold inspiration for a dorm room, a first home, a last home. They are a celebration of place, story, and joy.

Beyond structures, the blessing extends to those who travel and look through many windows. Great possibilities await us all—and those are blessed who get to travel to that promised joy from their own walls or gaze upon them out the window of their home.

The door is
marked,

It always means, "Welcome."

Home ...
a party

waiting
to
happen.

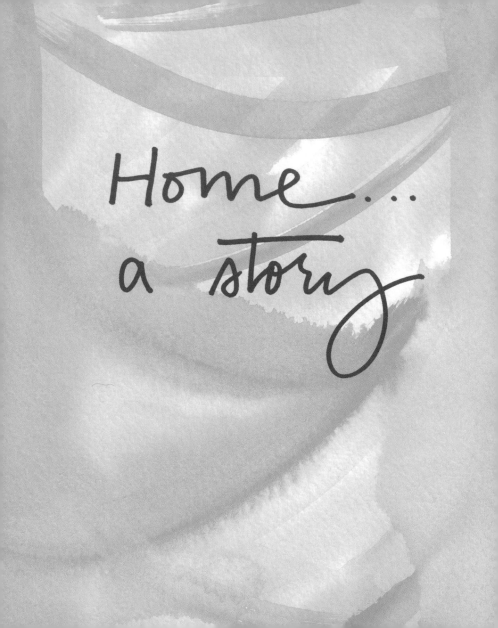

Home...
a story

waiting to be told.

waiting
to be
made.

Love
always
finds a way

to continue
the journey
home...

to the
comfort and
ease

found
on your
sofa,

to the
nourishment
and laughter

served
at your
table,

the sweetest
of dreams
sown in your
bedclothes,

the brightest
of fires
laid in your
hearth____,

the grandest of
festivities begun
in your kitchen,

to the
place
and
time

that enlivens
all your days.

May
your walls

each
room

hold laughter,

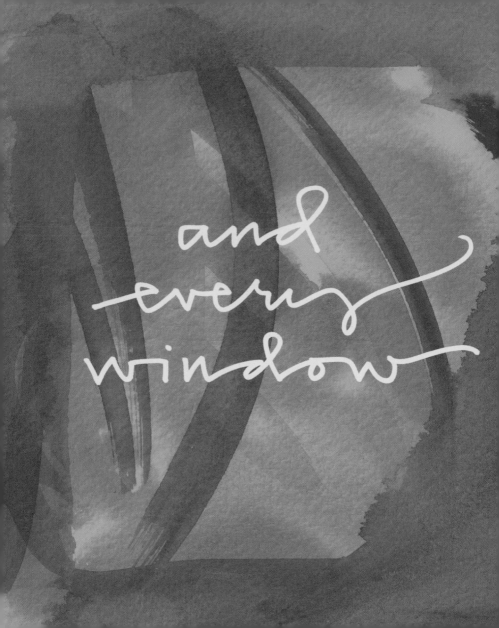

and every window

to great
possibility.

May home
be the
place

from which
you launch
your dreams.

may home
be the
place

from which
you go forth
and conquer

and return
to celebrate
and rest.

Under this
~~roof~~
may you
discover

the tools
to build
your
vision.

May you understand that these are more than just walls.

They make up
your safe and
good home.

May your date greet only friends.

May your
home
be furnished

with
hospitality
and
comfort.

May your
bed be made
with
tenderness

and forgiveness.

May the
lighted pathway
to your home

guide the footsteps
of good
fortune
and grace.

May you leave
your home
to share

all your
best qualities
with the world...

and as you
return may
you discover

the
better parts
of yourself.

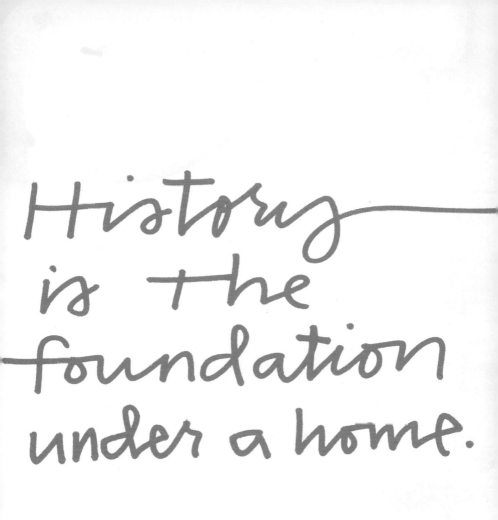

History is the foundation under a home.

Connections of family and friends are hands held across your table.

Welcome is always close to the door.

In the press
of all
the
lists
and "have to's"

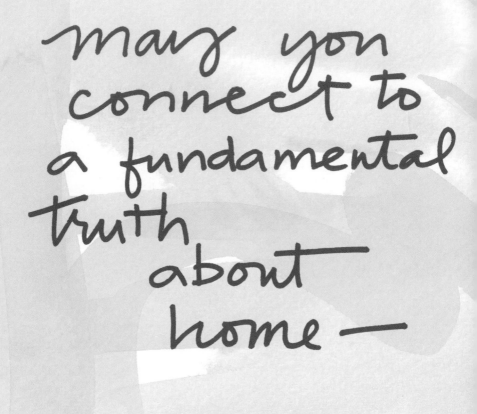

may you
connect to
a fundamental
truth
about
home —

it is
your own
sanctuary.

Admit to loving all the fuss and festivities, the planning, parades, parties, presents, and sweet memories.

Home is easy -

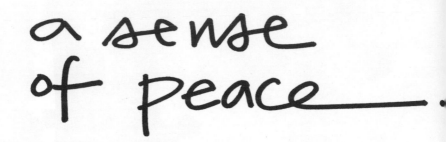
a sense
of peace _____.

Home is a
gentle release
from the
pressures of
the road.

Home
is where

you tend
a garden
and
hope grows.

Home
is where

you rearrange
a cupboard
to solve a problem.

you dare
to **dream** and
your harvest
exceeds your
greatest
& expectations.

Home is a canvas for creating.

Home is a
gift to be
opened
everyday.

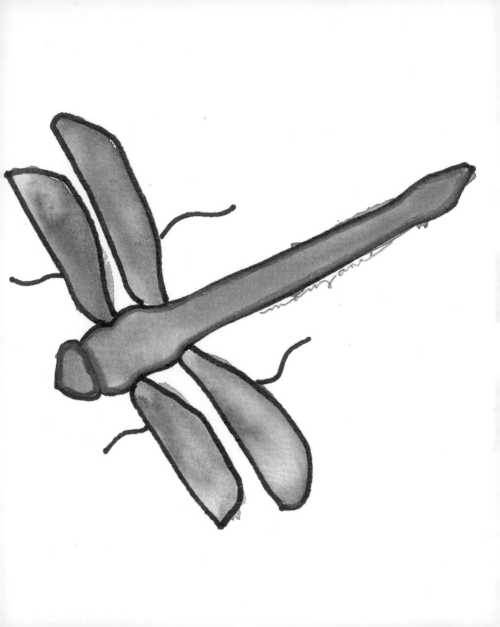

Home is
decorated with
the permission
to do nothing.

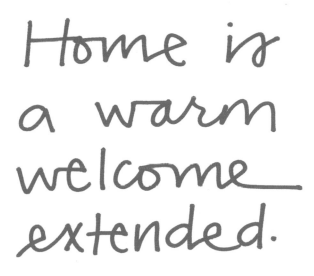

Home is
a warm
welcome
extended.

Home is
where
laughter
rolls
you off your chair.

Home is
where tears
have no shame.

Home is the whisper

of *promise*
that draws you back.

Home is
the place
where
love lives.